Guinea Pigs

*The Ultimate Beginner's Guide to Raising
Healthy Guinea Pigs for Life!*

Table of Contents

Introduction

I want to thank you and congratulate you for downloading the book, **"Guinea Pigs- The Ultimate Beginner's Guide to Raising Healthy Guinea Pigs for Life".**

This book contains proven steps and strategies for raising healthy guinea pigs.

Are you thinking of buying guinea pigs anytime soon? Do you want to know how to fix their living quarters? Do you want to choose the best possible supplies for your pets? This book will help you!

If you take the time to read this book fully and apply the information held within, this book will help you understand your responsibilities as a pet owner. You will learn about things that can help you provide your guinea pigs with the loving care that they need in order to live a long and comfortable life. You will become a more confident pet owner because you can make educated choices for your furry friends.

Guinea pigs are good starter pets for anyone who wants to learn how to take care of another creature. They can be warm, loving and comical. With the help of this book, you can experience the joy and fulfillment of raising and caring for guinea pigs. This book will help you enjoy the experience of having a pet. You might even start to breed guinea pigs someday!

Thanks again for downloading this book, I hope you enjoy it!

Chapter 1: Before Buying a Guinea Pig

Guinea pigs can be such lovely pets. They are small, cute and actually quite comical. They are wonderful creatures and they can easily provide entertainment for people of all ages. If they are cared for properly, they can be very tame. Once you win their hearts, you can easily treat them as lap pets. They'll happily munch on food as you stroke their hair. Some guinea pigs who receive proper care live for as long as six to ten years!

Typically, guinea pigs are considered as pets for children. Since they are so small, many assume that taking care of guinea pigs is easy. However, there are many things to consider if you want to raise guinea pigs. It's still a responsibility that you need to prepare for in any way you can.

It's important to keep in mind that guinea pigs are not toys.

Regardless of how small guinea pigs seem to be, they need constant care and attention from a responsible adult who can provide them with their needs. Children should never be allowed to care for guinea pigs without supervision. Guinea pigs are delicate creatures. They can appear fragile and nervous if they are unhappy in their environment. If they are uncomfortable, they might jump off when being handled. When they are suffering from a lot of stress, there's a good chance that they'll get hurt or injured. Before buying a guinea pig, you should first learn about their basic needs in order to ensure that your pets would receive the best kind of care.

Scientifically speaking, guinea pigs don't come from Guinea, nor are they considered pigs. They are from the species *Cavia Porcellus* from the family *Rodentia,* and they are believed to have originated from South America. There is a popular theory that they are called "pigs" because they grunt and squeal like pigs. "Guinea", an old English coin, was the price of a guinea pig when it was sold by British sailors in the 1600's. Hence the name "guinea pigs".

Do you think that guinea pigs are the right pets for you? Are you ready to give them attention and long-term commitment?

Here are some of the advantages of owning and caring for guinea pigs.

They are friendly and sociable

When tamed and cared for properly, guinea pigs can be extremely docile. They rare bite and they are very sociable creatures. Guinea pigs love interaction with other guinea pigs or with humans. In fact, a guinea pig with no companion is very likely to die easily. They have a "herd" mentality which always makes them seek companionship. Their natural instinct to gather and be with others is what makes them such pleasant pets.

They can be easily petted and trained. Given the proper stimulation, they can even be trained to do tricks! Since they are used to companionship, it is a bad idea to keep them in an isolated area of your home. Always make sure that you put them in a location where they can interact with the other members of the family. It would be best if you can get at least two guinea pigs so that they have each other a companions.

They are easy to care for

Perhaps many older children are given the responsibility to care for guinea pigs because they are considered easy to care for. All they need are the basics and they will survive. You don't need to buy a lot of equipment and you don't need a big space. Since they are small, they require little maintenance.

Generally speaking, all they need are fresh water, timothy hay, dry pellets and vegetables. Many owners invest in cages in order to give guinea pigs a controlled environment, but even their cages only need to be cleaned about once every two weeks. They shouldn't be bathed more than twice a year. Also, vet costs are often very low. The only regular grooming they need is clipping of nails once every three weeks.

They don't usually cause trouble

It can be such a pain to care for pets who can be destructive. Some really wild ones can even end up destroying your house! With guinea pigs, you don't have this problem. They are really small, so you can't expect them to create a lot of damage. It's not in their nature to bite or tear up our carpet. They are just too small, too fragile, too nervous and slow to create this kind of damage.

The greatest damage that they can do is pee and poop around your home. However, this can still be prevented by making sure that their territory is limited to a cage or to a small and controlled area. Some guinea pig owners claim that they have successfully litter trained their guinea pigs, but these cases are very rare.

Guinea pigs are not expensive

In general, pets are expensive to maintain. It's almost similar to having another child in your home. They have needs, and as the owner, it is your responsibility to provide.

If you are looking for an option that won't burn a hole in your pocket, guinea pigs are perhaps the best option for you. You don't even have to buy them! You can adopt guinea pigs from a shelter. There are a lot of guinea pigs who are looking for a home. Most shelters will even be willing to teach you how to care for your guinea pigs upon adoption.

Perhaps the only thing that would really cost you when buying guinea pigs is setting up their home. You'd have to invest in a cage and buy beddings. If you are really determined to save money, you can even opt to just make your own cage. This is ideal because you can customize the size and adjust the materials according to what will be most convenient for you. You also have to invest in beddings for your guinea pig's home. If you have extra cash, you can buy wood shavings for your guinea pigs. But as always, there are cheaper options, if you want something more affordable, you can invest in fleece instead.

As long as your guinea pigs don't get really sick, you won't really spend much on veterinarian visits. Also, food pellets are pretty affordable so you don't have to worry about feeding them. Once you settle them in their home and get their routines fixed, you won't need to shell out a significant amount of cash anymore.

They live long

For such small creatures, the life span of guinea pigs is pretty long. The average lifespan of guinea pigs is about four to six years, but if you give them first-class care, they might live for up to ten years! For comparison, rats and hamsters can live for only an average of about two to three years.

Also, even if they look small, nervous and fragile, they are not as sickly as other small pets. It's very unlikely that you'll suddenly find them sick dead. Overall, guinea pigs have stable lives. You don't need to constantly worry about their health and well-being.

Preparing for your guinea pig

Do you think that you are ready to buy or adopt guinea pigs anytime soon? Before you head to the pet store or adoption shelter, you must first prepare yourself for the responsibilities of owning a guinea pig. As the pet owner, it is going to be your responsibility to provide the guinea pigs with all their red such as food, grooming, exercise, and general care.

Here are some of the things that you should consider before bringing in a guinea pig into your home.

Check for allergies. It is a definite possibility for you and your loved ones to be allergic to guinea pigs. Before you commit to adopt or buy guinea pigs, you first have to make sure that you won't have any bad reactions when exposed to these creatures. It is also a good idea to check if you are allergic bedding materials like fleece, hay or wood shavings.

If you have small children living in your home, it is also a good idea to brief them about the guinea pigs. It is important for them to understand the responsibilities of having a guinea pig around. Children who don't understand the importance of taking care of a pet may subject the creature to torture without realizing it. It's important to give them an idea on how to care for the pet in the right way.

One of the most important things to do in order to avoid problems is to keep the living area of your guinea pigs clean and hygienic. Even if guinea pigs are relatively small pets, it is still important to make sure that their urine and droppings are cleaned often. This will ensure that you won't encounter health problems that can cause problems for you, your pet and your family. Keeping pig quarters clean means trying to develop a regular routine which will help you get rid of unwanted substances in the living area of your guinea pig. As you get to know your pet better, you will find it easier to figure out what routine works for you and your pet.

Read up on what possible health issues you should expect when raising guinea pigs so that you'll be able to take necessary steps to avoid health problems for you and your family. By knowing the possible health issues you can encounter in the future, you can prevent your guinea pig from acquiring various illnesses.

For example, one of the things that you should watch out for is obesity. Guinea pigs tend to eat a lot and gain excess weight. It is a good idea to control their food and to allow them to exercise for a few hours a day in order to ensure that their bodies won't balloon. There are also other things to watch out for like heat stroke, lung problems and dental problems. Keep in mind that you also have to ensure that they get good grooming. Constantly brush their fur to avoid mites and lice. Also, make sure to constantly trim their nails.

Chapter 2: Housing, Bedding and Cage Supplies

When buying guinea pigs, one of the first things that you should consider is their living area. Though they only need a small space, you should think about how to address their housing needs to ensure that they would receive proper care. Just like any other pet, guinea pigs deserve to receive the best possible housing that you can offer as a pet owner.

It is best to prepare everything before you even buy or adopt your guinea pigs. Here are some of the things which you might find helpful.

1.)Where will you get your cage?

This is probably the single greatest investment that you will make for your pet. You have three options: make the cage, buy the cage, or have the cage customized for you. Each option has its own advantages and disadvantages. It's all a matter of choosing which one suits your needs perfectly.

Making a cage is probably the cheapest but most time consuming option. When you make a cage, you can come up with the most efficient design even if you only invest on the materials. You don't need to spend much but you'll get exactly what you want... if you are a good carpenter. You need to have a background on carpentry to be able to do this successfully. You also need to set aside time to complete the project, so it's not ideal for someone with a busy schedule.

Buying a cage is probably the most convenient option because all you have to do is go to a pet supplies store, choose something you like, pay for it and go home. Unfortunately, buying a cage is probably going to be a bit pricey. Furthermore, your choices are limited to whatever is being sold in the pet stores, so you don't have the option to customize or personalize the cage.

Having your cage customized is probably the most expensive option, but you will likely get exactly what you want without wasting time. You have an expert who can help you get exactly what you want so you know that things will go smoothly. If you want to have your cage customized, it is important to choose a carpenter who can really help you with your project. Look around and choose well so that you can hire the one who can give you the best.

2. What should be the size and structure of the cage?

Guinea pigs require a minimum area of at least two square feet per guinea pig. Most cages sold in pet stores meet this requirement. If you have more than one guinea pig, just adjust accordingly. This means that if you have two guinea pigs, your cage should be at least four square feet and so on. Just adjust the size according to the number of guinea pigs that you plant to care for.

Also, one thing that you need to keep in mind is that guinea pigs don't like heights. They usually end up falling and hurting themselves in the process. To avoid accidents like this altogether, it is best to keep your cage at one level only. If you must make it multi-level, make sure that the levels are fairly close together to minimize injuries.

3. What material should be used in making the cage?

Generally speaking, plastic, metal or treated wood make good options for a guinea pig cage. It's up to your budget and preference which material would suit you best.

It is best to avoid glass. Aquariums do not make suitable homes for guinea pigs. An aquarium will make your guinea pigs feel nervous, uncomfortable and maybe even a bit claustrophobic. It does not allow for an efficient air circulation and it will also retain heat when left to sit under the sun for too long. It will also mean a lot of work for you. Aquariums are harder to clean when compared to other cage options.

Also be mindful if you choose to use a cage with a wire bottom. The legs of your guinea pigs might get stuck in the mesh bottom. Make sure that you cover up the flooring with solid flooring.

4. What should be the temperature of the cage?

To make your guinea pigs feel more comfortable, it is important to make sure that the temperature of their living quarters is ideal. Try not to make their environment too hot or too cold. However, it is useful to note that since guinea pigs originated from the high plains of South America, they can tolerate the cold fairly well. Watch out for signs of heatstroke if you choose to put the cage outdoors or if you live in an area where the temperature is above 80 degrees Fahrenheit. The most ideal temperature for guinea pigs is around 65 to 68 degrees Fahrenheit.

Beddings

Once you've chosen a cage for your pets, you must do what you can to make them comfortable. Beddings are used like carpets to line the bottom of the cage. They serve three purposes: 1. It can serve as the litter box of the guinea pigs, 2. It is where the guinea pigs can nest and burrow, and 3. It provides a soft flooring so that the guinea pigs can walk comfortably. When choosing material for your beddings, it is best to choose products that are okay to eat just in case your guinea pig accidentally eats them.

Here are some of the most popular bedding materials that you can purchase in the market nowadays.

1.)Cedar shavings

Cedar is actually not a good kind of material for beddings because it can cause problems in the respiratory system and the lungs. Also, there are several animals which may have allergies to cedar shavings. Most of the problems come from the aromatic oils that are used to mask the natural scent of cedar.

2. Pine shavings

Pine shavings are popular and easy to acquire, but they can cause the same problems as cedar shavings. Though it is a bit less harmful, it is also covered in aromatic oils which could be harmful to guinea pigs since they are exposed to the beddings 24/7. You must keep in mind that animals are more sensitive to smell than humans are so something that may seem harmless to you may actually harm your pet.

3. Aspen shavings

Aspen shavings are good because they come from a non-aromatic hardwood. Therefore, they don't contain harmful aromatic oils which can be unhealthy for your pet. The only downside of Aspen is that it does not have odor control capacity, so it is essential to always keep your cage clean.

4. Carefresh

Carefresh is a popular choice that is considered safe for pets. In general they are considered better than wood shavings. It has excellent odor-control qualities and generally does not promote ammonia formation

5. Paper-based beddings

Paper-based beddings usually offer excellent odor control and they are very convenient for the pet owner to prepare. However, it can feel a little rough for the pet. The best thing to do is to combine paper-based beddings with timothy hay to make the beddings more comfortable for your guinea pigs.

6. Corncob

Many pet owners also like using corncob as beddings, but they are not actually very suitable for pets. They are difficult to digest and they are also very prone to molds. This kind of bedding is not recommended.

7. Timothy hay

This is perhaps the best option you have for beddings since they are very convenient to use and they will make your pet feel comfortable. It is a natural food source that can be easily digested. It also has a pleasant smell which makes it safer for your pets. Unfortunately, timothy hay does not have effective odor control. Also, it tends to grow molds when left moist or wet. The best thing to do is to pair with paper-based beddings. Use timothy hay as the top layer and change it every two days to keep in hygienic.

Other cage supplies

Your pet is just like a baby. You need to prepare all the supplies you need to ensure that all their needs would be met accordingly. Fortunately, there aren't a lot of things which are needed for the daily living of these small creatures. It is a good idea to invest in high-quality supplies because it will make your life as a pet-owner much easier.

For feeding, you need to prepare a water bottle and a food dish. For the water dish, choose a style cannot be easily overturned so that the guinea pigs won't create a mess in the cage. This is the same reason why water bottles are preferred over water dishes. Water dishes can be messy and they can easily be contaminated with urine and droppings.

For entertainment, you might want to provide toys for your pet. Fortunately, toys for guinea pigs are affordable and very easy to acquire. These simple toys might save your pets from boredom. PVC pipes, rocks, tubes and bricks are perfect for your pet's amusement.

Chapter 3: Food and Nutrition

Because of their South American background, guinea pigs are used to eating grass, herbs and dandelions. They are strictly vegetarians so fresh greens should be available every day. Grass and hay play an important part in their diet because it helps keep their digestive systems functioning well. It also helps prevent vitamin C deficiency. Problems in vitamin C can lead to weak joints, weight loss and poor health in general.

Timothy hay is again the best option for feeding. It has a high fiber content so it is perfect for your pet's digestive system. Hay also provides a good way for your pets to exercise their chewing instinct. You can choose between a pre-packaged dried timothy hay or fresh hay. Both are usually available in pet or feed stores.

While guinea pig pellets are not ideal as the main source of nutrition for your guinea pigs, they are helpful as supplements. Guinea pig pellets are ideal supplements because they can give your guinea pigs a balanced dosage of vitamins, minerals and protein. However, pellets alone are not adequate because they don't contain vitamin C. Also, they don't contain fiber. Therefore, they won't really help in promoting a healthy digestive system. The best option is to mix fruits, vegetables and pellets. Ideally, 1-2 ounces of pellets are enough. Just add this serving to hay, raw vegetables and fruits.

When your guinea pig is new, it could be tempting to experiment with your pet's diet. However, try to introduce foods slowly to allow your guinea pig's digestive system to adjust.

Also, keep in mind that you should try to keep the servings of fruits and vegetables small. One grape or strawberry might seem nothing to you but it is actually more than enough for your guinea pig. Don't overfeed your guinea pigs. They have the tendency to get obese if they are always fed too much. When choosing fruits and vegetables, it is best to choose the ones which are high in vitamin C like kiwi, broccoli, apples, kale and tomatoes. Avoid feeding candy and dairy products to your guinea pig.

Water

Fresh drinking water should always be available for your guinea pigs. Without it, your guinea pigs might become sickly. Fruits and vegetables will provide some fluid for your pets but these are not enough to keep them healthy.

If you are worried that your guinea pig is not getting enough vitamin C, you can easily add supplements to their water. You just have to make sure not to put your pet's drinking bottle under direct sunlight because sunlight destroys Vitamins and takes away from the nutritional value.

Chapter 4: Reproduction and Health Issues

When it comes to the health of your guinea pigs, it is best to prevent any kind of sickness from developing. You can do this through good grooming and hygienic practices. A proper diet, a low-stress environment and sufficient exercise are essential in helping prevent illness of any kind.

However, even if you give your pets the best kind of care, it is still possible for them to get sick. When your guinea pig is sick, the best thing to do is to try to minimize the damage to your pet's body.

When guinea pigs are sick, they usually get very stressed. When you notice that your guinea pigs are lethargic, there is a good possibility that they are sick. You **should be concerned if your guinea pigs don't show interest in eating.**

Here are some sicknesses which are pretty common in guinea pigs.

Respiratory problems should be taken seriously because it can develop to become pneumonia. Respiratory problems are easy to spot. Some symptoms are difficulty in breathing and sneezing. In extreme cases, symptoms also include nasal discharge. The cause of respiratory problems is a virus called bordetella, a virus common in rabbits and dogs. Try not to house these pets in the same area as your guinea pigs.

Diarrhea is also a common problem for guinea pigs. It can be caused by eating too many vegetables, particularly greens. If you notice that your guinea pigs are showing signs of diarrhea, it is best to hold greens for a few days. If the diarrhea becomes worse, you should consult a veterinarian to avoid further problems.

Since guinea pigs don't handle heat very well, they are prone to heat stroke attacks. Because of the background, they generally don't handle heat very well, and they can die within minutes of overheating. To prevent heatstroke, it is best to keep your guinea pig in an area with a controlled temperature. You must also ensure that your guinea pig gets enough fresh water. If you think that your guinea pig is showing signs of heat stroke, wrap your guinea pigs in a towel soaked with water. You can also spray water on your guinea pigs to allow them to cool down. Pedialyte will help ease the situation but if you think that it's out of hand, it is best to check with your veterinarian.

You should note that broken teeth is actually a pretty common condition for guinea pigs. Their two front teeth can easily get broken when they fall off a high place or when they munch on something hard. Usually, their teeth will grow again in about two to three weeks. Your guinea pig might have difficulties in eating during the time when the new teeth are growing. During this time, it is important to ensure that your pet is receiving proper nutrition. You can chop the food and cut the hay into smaller pieces and so that it would be much easier for your pet to chew and digest the food.

If your guinea pig has an open wound, he or she is prone to catching bacterial or fungal infections. Clean the wounds of your guinea pigs to avoid complications and further infections. Use a hydrogen peroxide to clean the wound and follow up with a betadine solution daily.

Reproduction

While most people don't buy guinea pigs for breeding, it is a good idea to have a background on guinea pig breeding just in case. There are some cases where pet stores unknowingly sell pregnant females, and so you might find yourself suddenly needing to care for a newborn guinea pig.

In case you find yourself with a pregnant guinea pig, here are some of the things that you should know.

The gestation period for pregnant guinea pigs usually lasts for about 63-68 days. This gestational period is quite long compared to the other members of the rodent family because guinea pigs are fully developed when they are born. The average number of litter is about 2-3, but it some cases, there can be as much as six baby guinea pigs all at once. When they come out, they actually have fur and teeth! They can start eating a few hours after birth. However, even if they already seem "complete". They still need to get important vitamins from their mothers through nursing. Guinea pigs can nurse for up to three weeks. Keep in mind to separate males and females if you don't really have the intention of breeding guinea pigs. Females can start breeding when they are as young as five years old and males can start breeding once they reach eight weeks.

If you want to limit the number of pets you own, you might want to consider having your male guinea pigs neutered. If you have the luxury of space, you can just separate the males from the females to ensure that they won't breed.

Breeding

Non-breeding guinea pigs will live for a very long time, and they will likely live longer lives that the breeding ones. This is because pregnancy is very dangerous for guinea pigs. Since they are carrying overly developed youngs, the risk they need to bear is much greater than what other mammals do.

Breeding calls for mindfulness and educated choices. Research as much as you can to make breeding healthier and safer for your female guinea pig. A little research can go a long way. You will make the breeding experience better for your guinea pigs if you know what you are doing.

Here are some of the basic things that you need to know to help you decide if you are suited to breed guinea pigs

It is best not to breed your female guinea pigs who are younger than four months because it could put their lives in danger. Ideally, you should allow your female guinea pigs to reach the weight of around 500-600 grams before allowing them to breed. However, don't wait too long. Some females find it difficult to be pregnant after reaching 12 months of age. In this sense, it is essential to learn proper timing. Most experts learned to tell if a female is ready for pregnancy through experience. Learn how to observe basic guinea pig behavior in order to understand what they need and when they are ready for pregnancy.

Females are fertile immediately fertile right after giving birth, and two consecutive pregnancies are very stressful to their bodies. For their own safety, it is best to keep them away from males during this time to ensure that they won't get pregnant again. Ideally, there should be a 4-month rest between two pregnancies to allow the female guinea pig to be in a healthy condition before becoming pregnant again.

A female guinea pig may die due to complications after giving birth to a litter of babies. This can pose problems because newborn guinea pigs often need to be nursed. They need to receive nutrients from their mothers and food supplements may not be enough. Expert breeders are able to feed young guinea pigs by hand, but it takes skill to be able to do this efficiently. You might need the help of a veterinarian or an expert breeder if you want to learn hand-feeding as well.

Some experienced breeders claim that the smell of a birthing guinea pig causes other pregnant guinea pigs to deliver as well. This is a problem if the pregnancies are so far apart and the due dates are not close. This can lead to premature birthing of some of your female guinea pigs. In order to avoid this, it is best to separate the pregnant females who are due earlier than the others.

Unfortunately, there are mothers who can unknowingly and accidentally injure their young while giving birth. This usually happens when a mother use her teeth to help a young get out. In the worst cases, there can be damaged ears and toes. Unfortunately, parts that were lost can never grow back again. It helps to be present during birth to be able to control the injuries. To be honest, there is not much that you can do in relation to lost body parts. At best, you can just clean the wounds and bring the guinea pig to a vet to avoid any further complications.

Breeding guinea pigs can be a fun and fulfilling experience. It can be magical to see your pets increase in number. However, it can also be heartbreaking and tragic if you don't know what you are doing. Do not even attempt to breed hamsters if you feel that you are not yet competent enough to attend to their needs. You might end up handling them in the wrong way which could just result to problems in the long run. Before you even get into breeding seriously, try to learn as much as you can. There is nothing like hands-on training from experts. Also, if you want to really get into breeding, it is a good idea to start with taking care of guinea pigs as pets first. If you find that you are comfortable with the responsibilities associated with caring for guinea pigs, then you can level up and start breeding them as well.

Conclusion

Thank you again for downloading this book!

I hope this book was able to help you to understand the basics of raising guinea pigs.

The next step is to make a list of things that you need to do and buy in order to prepare for your guinea pigs. Don't rush the preparations. Take things slowly and surely to ensure that you are able to make the best possible choices for your pets. Read all the tips included in this book and conduct further research if you need.

Taking care of pets can be a fun and fulfilling experience, but don't forget that you have a lot of responsibilities as a pet owner. Make sure to do your job in order to keep your pets happy and healthy. One small mistake can lead to drastic consequences. You are just like a parent taking care of a baby! You need to take your responsibilities seriously.

Finally, if you enjoyed this book, please take the time to share your thoughts and post a review on Amazon. It'd be greatly appreciated!

Thank you and good luck!

Bonus Chapter – Choosing the Right Kitten

Often people assume that when it comes to choosing a kitten or a cat, unlike choosing the correct dog, it is quite easy. Although this is not as complex as choosing which breed of dog you would like there are still some questions that need to be asked.

First, you need to consider how long the kitten spent with its mother. Many people understand that a kitten is weaned within the first 8 weeks of life and therefore assume it is okay to begin adopting them out at that point, but research has shown it is best for a kitten to stay with their mother up to 12 weeks to ensure it does not develop such habits as finger sucking or sucking on other objects.

It is also important that the kitten stays with the mother for a longer period of time than 8 weeks to ensure it is able to socially develop, otherwise you may get a kitten or cat that wants nothing to do with you.

Second, you need to check the personality of the cat. Many people pick their kittens or cats based on color or design of the fur. This could not be more wrong to do. You see, maybe you really want a black cat, but find that the only black cats you can find are loners, they don't like to play and they don't like to be touched. In this case, you need to opt for a different cat.

You want to look for a cat or kitten that is playful and one who is confident if you have small children in the house. A timid kitten can be extra cute, but it may not be able to handle the environment in your home if you have small children.

See how the kitten reacts to you, get down on the floor and see if the kitten is afraid or you, if the kitten is well socialized it should be comfortable with you being there and not show fear.

Using something other than, your hand or finger see if you can get the kitten to play. It should be enticed and curious at the least.

You should also try to hold the kitten. Of then kittens and cats will squirm a little when being held by someone new but it should not hiss, scratch or bite at you. If it refuses to be held, you need to ask yourself if you are okay with having a cat or kitten that does not like to be held.

Ask questions about how the kitten has been raised. Often times if a kitten does not have human contact within the first seven weeks of life they will struggle to bond with them later on in life.

Once you have found a kitten or cat with a personality you like you need to have a vet check it out before you adopt it. This will ensure that there are not unpleasant surprises down the road. However, there are a few things you can look for on your own.

First, a kitten's fur should be soft and fluffy. There should be no bald spots and there should be no scabs or rashes on the kitten's skin. If you notice black specs of dirt in the kitten's fur, this is usually a sign that they have fleas. If you adopt this kitten, make sure to get it treated as soon as possible to avoid bringing the pests into your home.

Next, you need to make sure the kitten or cat is not too fat or skinny, a cats ribs should not be visible and if their stomach is swollen or hard it could be a sign that they have worms. This is treatable, but should be done immediately.

Check inside the kitten or cat's ears. If you see brown or black grit inside this is a sign of ear mites and needs to be treated as soon as possible.

Ask questions about what the cat has been eating; make sure she is eating solid foods before you adopt her. You should also check to ensure there is no sign that the cat or kitten has diarrhea. A dirty back end could be a sign of a sick kitten. Observe the kitten's energy level as well, if it seems sleepy or lethargic it could be suffering from illness.

Bringing Your Kitten or Cat Home:

Now that you have chosen your kitten or cat you want to make plans for bringing it home. It is best to plan to bring your kitten home when you have a few days off that you will be spending mostly at home so the kitten can get used to the new environment.

You have to remember if you have just adopted a kitten, it has just left its mom as well as its brothers and sisters, this is a big deal for a kitten and you should be there to help the kitten feel comfortable.

If you have other animals in the home or even small children, it is best to visit the vet before the cat is ever brought into the home. You don't want your new furry friend to bring in fleas or a sickness that could harm those already at home.

You should also make sure the new cat or kitten has a special small area that is all their own. It will take her a few days or even a week to get used to her new home and feel confident around the other animals. Therefore, even though they are sure to become the best of friends in the future, you need to make sure she can take the time she needs to get used to her new home and everyone who lives there.

You must understand that the kitten or cat may hide a lot in the first few days in the new home but this is completely normal. Give the animal the space it needs to get comfortable.

Made in the USA
Middletown, DE
30 November 2015